Revision and Exam Strategies

The *Student Essentials* series

Student Essentials: Critical Thinking
Student Essentials: Dissertation
Student Essentials: Essay Writing
Student Essentials: Exam and Revision Strategies
Student Essentials: Study Skills

STUDENT ESSENTIALS

Revision and Exam Strategies

Mary Wickham

trotman **t**

Student Essentials: Revision and Exam Strategies

This first edition published in 2011 by Trotman Publishing, a division of Crimson Publishing Ltd, Westminster House, Kew Road, Richmond, Surrey TW9 2ND

© Trotman Publishing 2011

Author Mary Wickham

Designed by Andy Prior

British Library Cataloguing in Publication Data
A catalogue record for this book is available from the British Library

ISBN 978 1 84455 416 4

Typeset by IDSUK (DataConnection) Ltd

Printed and bound in the UK by Ashford Colour Press, Gosport, Hants

Contents

Introduction

There are not many people who look forward to exams and revision but most accept that they are an important part of degree programmes. Some actually prefer exams to written assignments as once an exam is finished you can forget about it until results day, whereas with an essay or coursework, there always seems to be room for improvement. However, in order to achieve a top grade, you do need to plan your revision carefully so that you enter the exam hall feeling confident that you've prepared effectively.

Whether you'll be taking your first exams at university, or you're further along the path to your degree, you'll benefit from thinking through the revision process and the day of the exam itself. The revision period does not solely consist of sitting in a library with books in front of you. It requires that you look after yourself, that you choose the best place to study and that you plan carefully. The same goes for the exams themselves. There are strategies that you can adopt to help to make the hours spent sitting at a desk writing go as smoothly as possible. So help yourself to get through your exams with the least stress by thinking ahead, planning ahead and reading ahead.

Starting your revision early is another key to success. Research has shown that the earlier you start, the more you'll retain in your long-term memory. Although it can be tempting to spend the last day or two before an exam cramming, starting earlier will be much more beneficial. The best prepared students will be thinking about their exams long before the revision period starts and will have their notes in order and their files organised. But don't worry if that doesn't sound like you. The fact that you're reading this book shows that you're on the right track towards achieving a top grade.

In this book you'll find ways to plan your revision time so that your learning leads to long-term retention of the materials that you've been studying. You'll discover that effective revision allows you to have breaks from studying with time for other activities. Everyone has their own revision style, but that doesn't mean you should feel that there is no way of improving your personal revision style. You need to optimise your strategies and discover ways that help you to do this. By creating and following your individual study plan, you'll keep track of what you've completed and what still needs to be done. By using a range of revision resources, there is a smaller chance of boredom, meaning there is less chance of a lack of motivation. By following a plan and staying motivated, your mind will be focussed on the steps you should take to succeed when the exams actually start.

You can read the book from cover to cover or dip in to find some tips that will help with a particular strategy. However you use the book, you're certain to find information that will help you to improve your grades and reduce the stress that exams and revision can often cause.

PART 1

Before the exams: planning and revising

It's never too early to start planning for your exams and careful preparation can make you feel on top of your revision right from the word go. The first three chapters of this book will help you to get started by organising a revision timetable, finding revision resources that go beyond the books in the library and looking at the different styles of exams used in a range of subject areas. Whether you're a science, humanities, law or medical student, you'll find strategies and suggestions that will help you.

1 Getting started

One of the hardest things to do when you have exams looming is to actually start your revision rather than just thinking about it. Tidying your room or walking your dog suddenly seem like attractive activities even though you would normally avoid them like the plague! Even if you don't need extra encouragement to start your revision, it's still important to have a plan beforehand. In this chapter, you'll find information about important things to think about, such as setting goals and drawing up a revision timetable. First of all though, you need to give some thought to your priorities.

First things first

Before getting down to your revision, make the necessary preparations.

- Find the best place to study, make it comfortable and have everything you need with you: pens, paper, a drink and perhaps music, if you find music helps block out distracting sounds and allows you to focus. Make sure there's no TV, no access to emails and social networking sites, and switch off your phone.
- Organise and file your notes before revising from them. This is something you can do from the start of your course and will save valuable time when your revision timetable starts.
- Which topics need more revision than others? If you start with the difficult ones, you'll be encouraged and gain confidence as

you revise because the topics will get easier rather than more difficult, so schedule the difficult topics first.

Drawing up a revision timetable

A revision timetable can help you to use your time in the most effective and efficient way. It's all too easy to sit down to revise but then waste time deciding what to do, how long to do it for and then end up doing not very much at all! However, you also need to be realistic and not set yourself a schedule that's impossible to meet. So while you should not get carried away by designing an overambitious, beautifully presented timetable, it's worth thinking about how much you have to do before the start of your exams and putting together a realistic revision timetable to help you fit everything in.

Styles of timetables

There is not necessarily a 'one style fits all' version of a revision timetable. If you've never drawn up a schedule before, then it's worth using a template (like the one on pages 7–8) as a starting point and if this works well, you'll probably want to stick to a similar style in the future. Feel free to adapt this template so it works for you.

What to include in your timetable

There are some key questions to ask yourself when making a revision plan.

■ How long before the exams begin will your revision start? If you have an exam term, allow yourself a short break at the end of the second semester and get down to revision about six weeks before the exams start.

- What time of day are you most productive?
- Do you prefer to separate your revision topics or integrate them?
- How long can you concentrate on your revision before taking a break?
- Will your revision time be interrupted by other commitments, for example, an important sports competition or a friend's birthday party?

QUICK TIP

Whatever style of revision suits you best, it's important to have time for breaks and relaxation. Cramming for exams for long hours day after day is rarely the most effective strategy for achieving high grades. Too much study can be as unproductive as too little.

Using your answers to the questions above, you can create a template, find the times and dates of your exams and start planning.

You should also factor in:

- fixed activities such as a part-time job or a sports club – it's not necessary to give up everything else that you do
- revision sessions arranged by your college or university
- relaxation time and family activities.

If you find it difficult to concentrate for more than short bursts of time, start off with short periods of revision, for example 15 to 30 minutes at a time, include regular breaks and aim for longer revision sessions as you feel

QUICK TIP

Remember you can always make changes to your timetable and change the times at a later date if you feel that it's not meeting your needs. The timetable is designed to help you, not to hinder you.

more confident about your ability to concentrate. Give yourself a reward when you feel you've met your target successfully. This reward could be a chat with a friend, a computer game, some time on a social networking site, a tasty snack or a relaxing bath. Don't reward

QUICK TIP

Needless to say, alcohol doesn't work too well as a reward – you're unlikely to concentrate when you return to your revision later.

yourself when you don't deserve it! This means that you must stick to your revision timetable and only take breaks when they are scheduled.

When you're happy with your schedule, make a poster version and put it on the wall in your room. Then you can check your progress, see if you're sticking to your plans and make adjustments where necessary. For example, you might find that you're ready to increase the time you can study in one stretch or that you concentrate better first thing in the morning than you thought you would. On the other hand you might have a bad day or feel ill. You'll then need to make adjustments so that you can catch up, but don't get into a panic about it. Unless you miss several days in a row, adding an extra hour or two won't be a problem.

Revision timetable: example

Time slot	Mon	Tues	Weds	Thurs	Fri	Sat	Sun
9.00–10.00	Revise macro molecules1	Study group	Study group	Revise evolution	Revision at uni	Revise enzymes	Break
10.00–10.30	Break	Break	Break	Break	Break	Break	Break
10.30–12.00	Revise macro molecules 2	Revise genomes	Revision at uni	Revise evolution	Revision at uni	Revise enzymes	Break

12.00 – 13.00	Lunch	Sports	Lunch	Lunch	Lunch	Meet friend for lunch	Lunch
13.00 – 14.30	Revise immunology	Lunch	Revision at uni	Plan practice answers	Go to library	Revise DNA structure	Visit friend
14.30 – 15.00	Revise immunology	Revise genomes	Break	Plan practice answers	Go to library	Revise DNA structure	Go to library
15.00 – 17.00	Revise immunology	Revise genomes	Visit friend	Go to gym	Football	Revise DNA structure	Go to library
17.00 – 19.00	Dinner/ break	Dinner/ break	Dinner/ break	Dinner/ break	Dinner/ break	Dinner/ break	Dinner/ break
19.00 – 22.00	Review day's work	Review day's work	Look at past papers	Review day's work	Review day's work	Watch TV	Check week's progress and goals

Filing and organising lecture notes

If you're proactive from the start of your course, you'll already have a filing system that works for you and you'll be able to locate your notes easily. If you haven't been organised up to now, it's not too late. You can still sort out your notes carefully before starting your revision.

Hints and tips for filing

- Set up a filing system at the beginning of term, or arrange one before you start revising.
- Have a separate file for each module.

- Use different colours for your files so that you can locate what you're looking for quickly.
- Use file dividers for different topics.
- Date all your notes and number the pages so you can match them to the lectures easily.
- Use headings based on topics and make them stand out. When you're revising for exams you'll find what you're looking for much more quickly.
- Use a card reference system (a small box with notecards stacked alphabetically) from the beginning of your course to list books that you've found useful so that you can return to them for your revision. If you don't already use this system, start using one during your revision.
- Back up any assignments and notes on your computer with a memory stick. If you only have one copy and your computer crashes, they'll be gone forever.

A word of warning about highlighter pens!

Highlighters can be very useful as an aid to recognising important information in your notes. It's tempting to overuse them and feel that the more you highlight, the better the progress you're making with your revision, but in reality the highlighted sections become confusing. Have a system for using highlighters and then you'll find them a useful revision aid when you look back at your notes. For example, you could use one colour for quotations, another for key words and terms and another for important points. So that you remember what the colours mean later, have a key at the top of your notes as a reminder.

Setting goals

The whole point of revising is to achieve good grades in your exams so the number one goal of your revision is exactly that – a top grade! However, you'll also benefit from setting intermediate goals to guide you through your revision.

By setting yourself attainable goals you'll feel a sense of achievement when you reach them. Ticking off your goals from a list can be a real confidence booster and spur you on to complete your revision. Your goals can be incorporated into your revision timetable or pinned up somewhere you can see them easily to maintain your focus.

Some advantages of setting yourself goals:

- goals help you to push yourself
- goals help you to get organised
- goals help you to study more effectively as you're more focussed
- sticking to your goals helps you to avoid distractions.

Reward yourself each time you tick off one of the goals on your list and remember that people who set goals in their lives accomplish much more than those who don't, so setting goals now as a student will put you in line for further success when you finish your studies

Types of goals to think about:

- organising your notes before starting to revise
- reading sections of important texts and making sure you've understood them

- revising for a set period of time without succumbing to distractions
- sticking to your plan for each session on your revision timetable
- deciding when to take breaks and resisting the temptation to relax before reaching the set time.

Tips for top scores

- Exercise is a good way to start each day as long as it's not too strenuous. It wakes you up, stimulates blood flow to the brain and helps you to focus on your revision.

- Don't spend more time planning your revision than doing your revision. It's easy to get carried away with the *process* of revision rather than actually getting down to revision itself.

- Keep a non-caffeine based drink beside you while you're revising. Your brain is made up of 75% water and if you become dehydrated, your concentration will be affected.

✓ Dos	✗ Don'ts
✓ Remember that you still have a life beyond revision and that it's OK to phone your friends for a chat or arrange a game of football every so often.	✗ Give up if you have a bad day and cover very little from your revision schedule.
✓ Give yourself rewards, both big and small. When you get to the end of a stressful week, go out at the weekend.	✗ Schedule revision right through the night. Sleep is important.
✓ Make sure at the end of each day that you've covered what you intended to do, so that you keep track of your progress. If you need more time, you can make changes to your timetable.	✗ Make the mistake of thinking the first exam is more important than the others just because it's first.
	✗ Forget that the real world is still out there and you'll be back there before long.

2 Using revision resources

Students today have a variety of revision resources to turn to before important exams. However, the resources available must be used with forethought so as not to waste time. Therefore, before rushing to the library to take out lots of books or trawling through scores of online journals, think carefully about choosing resources that are readily available, and at the same time suit your needs. A little careful planning will help you to achieve top grades.

Identifying the subject areas

How much knowledge of your subject areas do you already have and what resources will you turn to in order to be better prepared than you are now? The most important resources will be:

- reading lists
- lecture handouts
- your own lecture notes
- revision and course notes on the virtual leaning environment
- the course outline given to you at the beginning of the module
- essay titles and coursework topics
- the assignments and coursework that you've written.

These resources help you to identify the subject areas to revise based on information from your tutors and past exam papers. It's impossible to revise every topic for every exam so you must start with a clear idea of how you'll narrow it down.

Past exam papers and assignment topics

There are three common ways of accessing past papers.

1. The university or college library.

2. Virtual learning environments (VLEs). Virtual learning environments are used by universities and colleges to provide access to useful learning materials and resources online. Common VLEs include Blackboard and WebCT.

3. Online. Your university or college website will usually have a library site that allows you to find past exam papers using your usual log-in details.

Past exam papers can be one of the most useful resources when you're preparing for exams. They help to give a focus to your revision and guide you towards topics that you need to revise. However, a word of warning is needed here! You should not use past exam papers to try to work out the precise nature of the questions that will be included in **your** exam paper. The syllabus could have had changes made to it that you might be unaware of. You can also get a false sense of security by thinking that a question in your real exam looks the same as one from a past exam; just a few changes to the words could mean a different response is required. One of the most useful ways to use past papers and assignment topics is to learn to recognise framing words and the different answers these words require.

Recognising framing words in exam questions

These are the words and phrases that tell you how you should approach the question. You'll probably be familiar with them from your coursework assignments but you may not have seen them all before. It's most important to follow these framing words carefully when answering questions. They will help you to engage with the topic and to understand how the examiner expects you to answer the question.

In the box below, you'll find some of the framing words that are used in exam questions. Make sure you understand what each framing word is actually asking so that they can guide you, both in the planning and writing of your answer.

Framing word	Definition
analyse	examine methodically and in detail
comment on	express an opinion supported by evidence
compare and contrast/critically compare	look at the similarities and differences in a critical way
discuss	write about in detail, taking into account different ideas and opinions
evaluate	assess usefulness or effectiveness
illustrate	explain or make something clear by using examples
justify	show to be right using reasons and facts
outline	give a summary of the key points

Framing word	Definition
relate	give an account of
review	write a critical appraisal of
interpret	explain the meaning of the topic in the context of the question
describe	give an account of the topic with all the relevant detail
examine	investigate thoroughly
trace	give an outline of the development
How far do you agree . . .	Discuss both sides of the argument and assess which is stronger . . .
What do you understand by . . .	How would you explain . . .
What are the implications of . . .	What are the possible effects or results of . . .

QUICK TIP

Remember: descriptive essays are rarely what the examiner is looking for. If the word 'describe' is used in a question, there will probably be another part of the question that includes a word that requires more evaluation, such as 'evaluate' or 'discuss'. Spending time analysing the question before starting to write is an important step towards achieving a top grade.

Use the framing words to devise new questions

You can use questions from past papers to devise questions of your own on a different topic. You can then plan answers for the questions you've devised. You'll usually find that similar words are used from one year to the next and your new questions are a useful way to focus your revision. Look at the example below from a geography exam paper.

Topic – squatter settlements

> **" Discuss the reasons** for the growth of squatter
> settlements and **comment upon** the positive and
> negative features of these informal settlements. **"**

The words in bold are the framing words for this question. By using a combination of framing words, questions from past papers and the topics that you've been revising, you can devise new questions that will help you prepare plans for practice answers.

The question below uses the same words as the question above for a different geography topic, showing how you can use the same 'frames' to come up with more questions of your own.

Topic – population growth

> **" Discuss the reasons for** the growth of population in
> China over the past 100 years and **comment upon** any
> significant trends that have occurred. **"**

QUICK TIP

If there are any questions that you don't understand, write them down and ask your course tutor, either personally or by email, to explain how you should respond to them. The topic will usually be clear but it may be that you don't fully understand the 'framing' words. You'll feel more confident in the exam if you can understand both the topic of the questions and how you should respond.

Conducting your own mock exam

Past papers can also be used to practise the timing of your answers as long as you really do pretend that you're in the exam hall taking the exam. It's best to tackle the questions in this way once you've completed most of your revision. You must stick to the instructions on the exam paper; it's no good setting yourself a time limit and then going to get a cup of coffee in the middle! So before sitting down to answer a question, go to the toilet, have something to eat and drink, and think of this as a good opportunity to have some realistic exam practice.

Follow these simple 'rules' during your exam practice.

- Choose a question with a topic that you feel you've revised for thoroughly.
- Analyse the question.
- Think about what the examiner is looking for.
- Make a plan.
- Produce a logically developed argument that goes beyond description.
- Structure your answer with an introduction, body and conclusion.
- Handwrite your answer. Your hand and arm can tire easily and this can lead to illegible writing so practise now before the real exams.
- Check for accurate grammar and spelling.
- Don't exceed the time you allocated for the question.
- Try and leave at least five minutes to read through your answer.

Soon after you finish writing, make a note of the points from the list above that you found difficult and what was relatively easy. Divide these notes into two parts, one concentrating on the practical aspects, such as timing, and the other on the 'academic' aspects, such as developing an argument. Focus on these points when writing more practice answers under exam conditions.

Revision periods

In many universities and colleges, there is a revision week timetabled into the semester. During this period, there may be classes during which tutors run over the important topics that you've covered during the year and answer questions from students. There may also be an appointment system to enable you to arrange to see your tutor and ask for specific advice. Check on the departmental noticeboards and read all of your emails so that you don't miss any of these important sessions.

Choosing what to read

When you're writing a coursework assignment you have time for in depth reading before you start writing and you have a list of relevant books to read. Exams are different. You don't have one topic and one reading list. You have all of the topics you've covered in the past year and many sources to choose from. This means that you might not be able to read as much as you'd like to, even if you've started your revision well before the exams, so you need to work out in advance what you're going to read.

Course outline

The course outline that was given to you at the beginning of the course will be invaluable. You can match up the topics with your lecture notes and handouts.

Next divide the topics into groups:

- those you feel that you understand well
- those that you have a reasonably good grasp of
- those that you find more challenging.

If you've started your revision in plenty of time, you can aim to revise topics from all three groups, but don't be too ambitious. If you spend too much time on the topics you find most difficult, you might still end up feeling that these topics are best avoided in the exam.

Reading lists

Based on the topics you've chosen, go through your reading list and select texts which you find accessible and which will provide you with a discussion of the key points without going into too much detail. You'll know which books you've found most useful during the year so don't try to cover too much new ground. Stick to the tried and trusted sources and have questions in mind while you're reading. If the information is not relevant, skip it and move on. Don't read the books from cover to cover. Always remember that you're revising for exams and that your reading should be a review process.

Add notes from these texts under the key topics that you've selected from your lectures. Use colours and highlighters to help you find the most important points when you return to your notes just before the exam.

Course assignments

Your course assignments are definitely worth having another look at. You'll see what the marker liked and didn't like about your work. Read the comments and feedback sheet carefully. If you cannot understand what any of the comments mean or why your grade didn't meet your expectations, now is the time to make an appointment with your tutor to discuss what you could have done differently. If you received a good grade, make sure you understand what your strengths are. You should also check the titles of the questions that you didn't choose for your assignment to gain further clues as to what may come up in the exam.

Knowing what an examiner wants: marking criteria

In most universities and colleges, there will be a list of assessment or marking criteria that tutors follow when allocating grades to exams and essays. If you haven't seen the marking criteria for your courses, find out about them. They are usually presented in percentage bands. Use them when you've written a practice answer to an exam question and see if your answer corresponds to the points needed to achieve a top grade. You could also talk to your tutor about the marking criteria to make sure that you really understand how they will be used.

Tips for top scores

- Before you go to see your tutors for advice, write down specific questions related to your revision. They will give more useful feedback if they can see you're taking your exams seriously.

- It's a better use of your time to plan answers from practice papers rather than write complete answers every time. After studying a topic, find an exam question from a past paper related to that topic and plan your answer. Closer to the date of the exam, choose one of the plans and write up a complete answer to the question.

✓ Dos	✗ Don'ts
✓ Make use of all the resources available to you.	✗ Forget that the information given by tutors in revision week can help to clarify problems you've had when revising.
✓ Revise the list of framing words before the exam as they give insight into how to respond to the questions.	✗ Choose which question to answer based only on the topic – make sure you understand what the framing words are asking and how to respond.
✓ Match the topics in the course outline with your lecture notes to make sure you know exactly what you should be revising.	✗ Waste time reading entire chapters of books that are not really relevant – choose what to read carefully.

3 Types of exams

More often than not, university and college exams conjure up images of writing essay style answers under strict time constraints, but exam styles vary from department to department. A law exam, a maths exam and a dentistry exam, for example, will all have features specific to their discipline. It's important to remember that different types of exam can require different styles of revision.

Different subjects, different exam styles

The style of the question paper and what you're asked to do can depend on the subject of your degree.

Humanities

Exams in the humanities are likely to focus on essay style exam answers. In this case, you'll usually only have to answer two or three questions in a two to three hour exam and each answer is normally worth the same number of marks.

QUICK TIP

Don't make the mistake of assuming you know what format your exams will be in. Term exams, for example, might be different from final exams. Always check with your tutor so that your revision is targeted towards the right type of question.

Here are some examples of essay style questions in humanities exams.

> " *Compare and contrast Anglo-American relations during the Suez Crisis and the invasion of Iraq.* "

> " *Consider the relevance of dreams and the interpretation of dreams in any two nineteenth century novels.* "

Sciences

Exams in science subjects often have questions on one topic broken up into short questions with different marks allocated to each part. There are usually three or four parts to each question. In this style of exam, allocate your time particularly carefully so that it corresponds to the number of points each part of the question is worth. The rule of thumb is *the higher the score, the more time you should spend*. This type of question often uses words like 'identify', 'explain' and 'define'.

A short answer question from a medical science exam is given below.

> *Compare the structure and composition of the aorta and a peripheral conduit artery such as the radial.*
> **[10 points]**
> *How do their structure and composition change with age?*
> **[5 points]**
> *Suggest one or more causes for the observed changes.*
> **[10 points]**
> *What is the relationship between the structural changes and the pathogenesis of so-called isolated systolic hypertension?*
> **[25 points]**

This type of short answer question is also used in business studies and engineering exams.

Law

Law exams can include case studies. You'll sometimes be allocated time to read the case study. You need to apply the knowledge that you've gained from your revision to the situation described in the case study.

Here is a typical case study question.

QUICK TIP

Look at past papers to get an idea of the different lengths and types of questions used in your department for case study questions.

Sarah and Alan are flat-sharing students. When Sarah is out shopping, she takes some perfume from a counter and puts it into her pocket. She sees a silk scarf that costs £40, changes the price-tag for one marked £20 and pays the lower price. Alan gives Sarah £40 for the electricity bill. Sarah uses the money to buy scratch cards but wins nothing. Sarah buys a CD and pays for it with a £10 note. The assistant gives her change for a £20 note by mistake. Sarah realises after she has left the shop but keeps the money.

Alan takes Sarah's health club season ticket from her room and returns the ticket three months later just before the membership needs to be renewed. Alan sees an exam paper on his lecturer's desk. He makes a photocopy and leaves the original on the desk.

Discuss the criminal liability for theft of Alan and Sarah.

Case studies are also used in business, psychology and medical exams.

Multiple-choice exams

Multiple-choice exams require you to memorise key facts and theories and to apply them to the question before selecting an answer. This may seem an easier style of exam at first glance but the drawback is that you're either right or wrong. You don't have any chance to show the examiner the thought process that you went through before selecting your answer. Therefore, your final grade depends entirely on the ticks in the boxes.

There are a number of key steps to take when answering multiple-choice questions.

■ Read the instructions very carefully. It's important to know whether to use a pen or a pencil. If a pen is required, you may also be instructed to use a pen of a particular colour. If you need to shade the correct box using a pencil, take two sharpened pencils to the exam in case one breaks. It's crucial to use the specific pen or pencil required or the scanner picking out the correct answers may not be able to read the mark that you've made on the paper. Imagine thinking you've answered all the questions correctly and then discovering you've been awarded a score of zero because the reader didn't register anything!

■ Timing is just as important as in written exams. Spend too long on a particularly difficult question and you might find yourself with insufficient time to answer the last few questions. These could be the questions that you understand well and expect to pick up full marks for. Therefore set yourself a certain amount of time for each question and stick to this. If you can't answer the question in the time you've allocated, move on, but remember to write down the numbers of any questions you've missed so that you can return to them later. If there are 20 questions to answer in one hour, allow yourself two minutes for each question and move on when two minutes is up. In this way you'll have 20 minutes left at the end to read through your answers and tackle the difficult questions.

- Read each question very carefully so that you spot words that might confuse you. You should highlight the important words and phrases, especially if they could catch you out. Think about the considerable difference between phrases like *Which of the following **best describes** . . .* and *Which of the following **does not describe** . . . .*

- Read each answer very carefully before making your final selection. In the tense atmosphere of the exam hall, it's easy to think you've spotted the correct answer without reading all of the options carefully.

- Avoid the temptation of changing your mind when you check your answers, unless you notice that you misinterpreted the question. More often than not, the first answer that is selected is the correct one.

- Unless you lose points for selecting an incorrect answer (known as negative marking) answer all the questions even if you have to guess.

Unseen texts used in exams

In subjects such as English literature, modern languages, history and philosophy, you may need to analyse a text from a source you've never seen before. However, this won't be the first time that you've experienced an analysis of this type. You'll have also discussed and critically analysed similar texts in class. Some students think that they don't need to prepare for this style of exam. This is far from the case. You need to look back over similar texts that you've analysed in seminars and ensure you're familiar with the techniques that your tutor has suggested. You'll really build up your confidence for this type of exam if you work with other students and analyse unseen texts together.

These are some of the points that the examiner will expect you to make:

- provide a context for the text
- identify and consider the most important ideas
- find evidence to support your ideas by using quotations from the text
- give an imaginative response that includes critical judgement and a personal reaction.

If you're studying for an exam with unseen texts, you can use the ACTIONS strategy to analyse the text. This strategy is especially useful for history exams but can also be used to help you start analysing sources for other subjects.

The ACTIONS acronym stands for:

Authorship
Context
Trustworthiness
Information given
Other sources
Not mentioned
Summary

Analysing the text using this strategy will ensure that you've covered all the key points.

Open book exams

Open book exams can seem like an easy option; if you can take your books into the exam, it won't really matter if you've forgotten some of the key facts and theories! However, this can be a disadvantage as well as an advantage. The examiner will be less likely to make allowances for slight inaccuracies and will expect a carefully considered response that is both succinct and relevant. If you have to spend too long referring to the books, your answer is unlikely to be either of these. Therefore, you must be really familiar with the relevant sections of the book through careful reading of the texts before the exam. You could have either essay style questions or short answer questions in open book exams, so be prepared for both.

Here are a few things to consider when taking an open book exam.

- If you've prepared well, you'll only need the book(s) as support and/or for references.
- Your memory skills are not being assessed so pay particular attention to theories, supporting arguments and analysis.
- Use 'stickies' or cards to mark the pages that you think you're most likely to refer to during the exam, but check in advance that you can have these in the exam.
- It's tempting to overuse quotations when you have the book in front of you. However, the examiner would like to see how you're able to use the texts, not that you can re-write the book! Therefore, limit the length of your direct quotations to three to five words in length
- Keep the initialism ASEA in mind when writing your answers. It will help you to avoid being too descriptive. This is particularly important in open book exams. There's no point in describing something that is described in the book!

A – Apply the information in the texts to the question.
S – Synthesise the arguments by combining and discussing key elements from both sides.

E – Evaluate the evidence.
A – Analyse the texts, don't just describe what they say.

Oral exams

The two most common types of oral exam are vivas and language exams.

A viva, or *viva voce*, is traditionally an oral exam based on your undergraduate or postgraduate thesis. However, it can also be used as a way to check if an undergraduate essay has been plagiarised. If you're going to have a viva, you'll be given details of the format well before it takes place and your supervisor will advise you on your preparation. An undergraduate viva will normally last between 30 minutes and an hour but a postgraduate viva will be considerably longer.

You must prepare thoroughly for the viva. The points below can be used to assist you in your preparation.

- You'll need to show your knowledge of the subject so read your essay or thesis very carefully beforehand and try and predict questions that could be asked.
- Practise answering the questions with a friend if you're not used to talking about your work.
- In the viva, listen very carefully to the questions and ask the examiner to repeat a question if you don't fully understand it.
- Don't answer questions with 'yes' or 'no'. The examiner wants you to justify your ideas and show your knowledge.

In the case of oral exams taken as part of a foreign languages degree, the following points are important.

- Make sure you have all the preparation materials provided by your tutor. These will usually be reading texts for discussion in groups or with the examiner.
- Remember you won't get any marks if you reply to all the questions with 'yes', 'no' or any other one- or two-word expressions. You must **engage** with the examiner.
- Practise with a friend on the same course or, even better, a friend who speaks the language that you're studying.
- If you have access to a language lab, check the self-study times and use the lab to practise. You have the chance to rewind and listen to yourself until you're happy with the end result.

Tips for top scores

- Short answer questions require succinct answers so that you don't waste any time. Practise writing short answers that get to the point quickly.

- In preparation for open book exams, concentrate on how you'll explain the text as you don't need to memorise it. Write down questions for yourself and ask a friend to ask you them so that you're sure you can communicate your answer effectively. It will then be easier to do the same thing when you're writing.

- Discuss case study questions from past papers with friends. You could even try having a role-play to help you to look at the situation from all sides.

- When revising for a multiple-choice test, concentrate on learning key facts, terms and definitions.

- If you have an oral for a foreign language exam, listen to radio programmes on the internet in the language you are studying. Listening skills are just as important as speaking skills in an oral exam.

✓ Dos	✗ Don'ts
✓ Check what you can and cannot take into open book exams.	✗ Think that an open book exam is an easy option that doesn't need as much preparation.
✓ Find out when you can use a language lab to practise for an oral exam.	✗ Spend too much time on individual questions in multiple-choice exams. Move on if you get stuck.
✓ Doublecheck your answers in a multiple-choice exam in case you've copied them incorrectly from your rough answer paper.	✗ Forget to check how many marks each part of a short answer question is worth.
✓ Make sure you allocate your time appropriately in short answer questions.	✗ Answer questions in oral exams with only a few words.

✓ Check how many answers you need to write in an essay exam. This can vary from subject to subject.	✗ Respond to a case study question without relating it to specific points from your course.
✓ Read case studies very carefully before starting to write your answer.	

PART 2

An individual approach

Now that you're ready to get down to the hard work that revision necessarily involves, it's important to remember that you and your friends will all have different ways of revising effectively. When it comes to exam preparation, there isn't a 'one style fits all' approach. You're an individual and you need to think carefully about what suits you. In the next three chapters, **you** are the focus. From what to eat to the amount of sleep you need, these chapters will help you to discover your own personal revision style.

4 Revision strategies that suit you

To really make sure that your revision is working for you, you must have an active approach. Many students revise using a passive style, which usually consists of reading and making notes from their reading but not doing much more. In this chapter you will find different strategies to help you revise more actively. Try them out and see which work best for you.

Making notes

It's easy to sit and make notes from a pile of books you've taken from the library and feel that you're making good progress with your revision. You can look back at these notes at the end of a revision session with pride. Or can you? If you're not careful, taking pages and pages of notes from books in this way can turn into passive revision and you'll find that these lengthy notes make it difficult for you to identify the key points when you return to them later. They can simply repeat what you've read. Instead, try using an active means of note-taking to help produce notes which will be more useful later.

The benefits of active note-taking

Active revision requires more than filling a notebook with notes. Notes are important but you should devise techniques that activate the notes and help them to become part of your long-term memory.

First, remember to keep all your notes on the same topic together. You don't want to find that you have lecture notes, notes from books and notes from seminars and tutorials all on the same topic but in different places. Active organisation can be started well in advance of the exams themselves – keep all your files in order from the first week of term. Make sure you have enough files, one for each topic.

How to be an active note-taker:

- write key questions for yourself on the topic that you're revising as you go along
- put your notes away and turn to the questions when you feel confident that you've made progress with your revision
- use bullet points to list your responses to the questions and if you notice gaps in your knowledge, go back to your notes for more revision.

> **QUICK TIP**
>
> You should be a note-maker, not a note-taker. Note-makers select, interpret and summarise; they think before writing notes and this aids understanding. Note-takers only read and copy.

While you're reading, remember that you need to be able to use the information in exam questions which ask you to discuss and analyse, not just describe. Annotate your notes with words that help you to do this.

The chart below has some examples of words which you can use to annotate your notes.

Words to use in notes	When to use the words
link	When you find points in the text that are closely connected use a highlighter pen to identify the parts of the text and write 'link' to show the connection.

Words to use in notes	When to use the words
explore	You can write 'explore' to indicate a point that you need to find out more about in order to have a wider knowledge of a topic.
use	'Use' identifies a key point that you feel will be very useful in the exam.
interpret	Sometimes you will find information that you need to explain to yourself so that the meaning becomes clear. Write 'interpret' on your notes to remind you to do this.
reflect	Write 'reflect' to indicate points that you need to return to later and think more deeply about.
develop	When you identify an important argument, write 'develop' to remind you to return to this point and give it deeper thought.

Different styles of notes

There are different styles you can use when making notes and of course you should choose the one that suits you best. However, you could experiment with different styles rather than just sticking to one you've always used. When choosing, remember you'll have to return to the notes later. Will you still remember your thought process when you made the mind-map? Are the key points clear in your linear notes?

Linear notes

Linear notes follow the order of the points from your reading. They take the form of lists or short sentences, laid out in a clear structure. They are effective when they use headings, indentations, bullet points and clear sub-sections. The more cluttered they become, the less effective they will be.

Example of linear notes

Electoral systems

1. First-past-the-post

Advantages:
a)   simple for voters
b)   no hung parliaments
c)   coherent opposition in parliament

Disadvantages:
a)   small parties gain few seats
b)   candidates win seats with less than 50% of vote
c)   may not reflect changes in public opinion

Mind-maps

Mind-maps suit learners who feel comfortable when using images to remember key points. They help you to visualise the connections between points in your reading. You start with the topic that you're revising and from this you use branches for the main points and sub-points. It's important not to use too many words as these will distract you and the impact of the image will be impaired. Take a look at the example on page 41 to give you an idea of how your mind-map should look.

You could even make your mind-maps into posters and put them on the wall in your room. If you use different colours, the key points will be reinforced more effectively. Keep pens handy so that you can add more branches and sub-branches as your revision progresses.

Figure 1: Mind-map for an essay question on intelligence

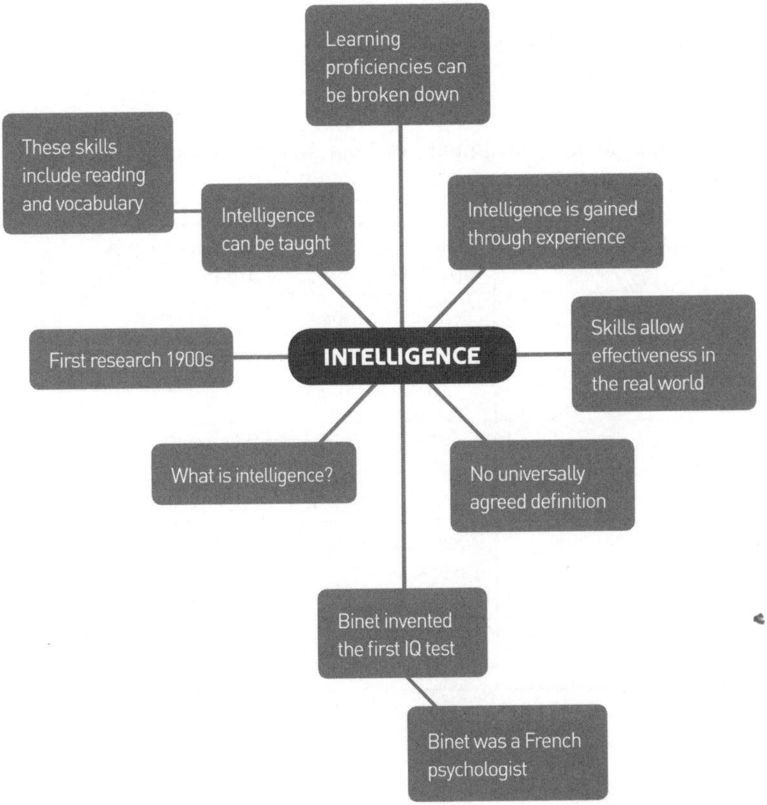

Tables

Constructing a table is another way than you can revise actively.
Tables can be used to condense longer notes in order to focus on
the key points more easily.

**Example of a table: impact of high speed rail link – London
to Birmingham**

General points	Impact on Birmingham	Impact on rural areas
Travel time between London and Birmingham cut to 49 minutes	Creates new jobs	Homes will be destroyed
Overall cost predicted at £33 billion	Increase in average wage	Will ruin beauty and tranquillity of countryside
Reduced congestion on roads	Businesses welcome the link	50,000 could be affected by noise pollution
Reduced carbon emissions		130,000 could be affected by vibration

Flow charts

Flow charts are useful when you want to show a sequence of
events, or a cause and effect relationship, for example when
explaining how a scientific process works. When preparing for a
law exam, flow charts are useful for revising cases and precedents.
The chart on page 43 explains the process for making glass.

Example of a flowchart

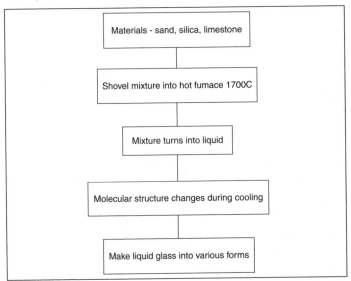

Materials - sand, silica, limestone

Shovel mixture into hot fumace 1700C

Mixture turns into liquid

Molecular structure changes during cooling

Make liquid glass into various forms

QUICK TIP

Remember: when you're making notes using any of the styles mentioned above, always use your own words. First, your own words show that you've thought carefully about the text and understood it. Second, this will help you to avoid unintentional plagiarism.

Using notecards

After making your detailed notes, you could put the keywords or summaries onto notecards that you can then take with you and review on bus and train journeys or at other times when you have a few moments to spare. Sometimes these 'short bursts' of revision give your memory an extra boost, but remember you need regular breaks from revision, so don't overdo it. If you have too many notecards to carry around with you, shuffle them up and take a random selection (but remember to put the topic on the reverse of each card, so you can identify which facts relate to which topic). In this way, you'll gradually reinforce many of the dates, formulae, quotes and key facts for your exams.

Another way to stay focussed before the exams is to put 'stickies' in strategic places around your flat or house. You'll see these regularly and you can carry on your revision while cooking, cleaning and getting ready for the day ahead.

Studying with friends

There are a number of advantages to forming study groups to help with your exam revision. The most important is reassurance. When you spend day after day sitting in your room or the library revising on your own, you might worry about your progress and whether you're concentrating on the most relevant topics. So be proactive and think about the ways that a study group can help you. If it's too late to do this, just get together with a few friends and chat through your experiences together.

Study groups

First of all, remember that the group is not meeting for your benefit alone. Not only will you gain support and feedback from the group but they'll be looking for the same from you. You must see yourself as part of a team. This means that you should work with friends who feel comfortable together.

If you decide that studying in a group will help you, decide early on who'll be in the group and how often you'll meet by contacting people who you've worked well with during the year by email or by talking to them after a tutorial. At your first meeting, use the list below to establish the rules and format of your study group but don't spend too long doing this as the main point of the group is to study!

- **Group rules.** Suggestion: if someone is speaking, they should be allowed to finish without being interrupted.
- **Aims of the group.** Suggestion: everyone has to commit themselves to cover one revision topic and fix the date for it.
- **Responsibilities.** Suggestion: someone leads the group in order to focus the discussion, perhaps the person who has covered the revision topic that week.
- **Agreeing deadlines.** Suggestion: decide what you want to cover in the time available and stick to it.
- **Checking on progress.** Suggestion: every week one member of the group takes brief notes to make sure the original plan for the discussion was adhered to.
- **Evaluating performance.** Suggestion: do this quickly to make sure it doesn't use up valuable revision time.

Once you've decided on the format of your group you can use strategies from the list below to help you cover all of your revision topics.

> **QUICK TIP**
>
> Remember that it's up to the members of the group whether to run the group in a formal or informal way.

- Choose a question from a past exam paper and discuss the key points needed to respond to the question.
- Divide a text into topics and read these at home, making notes on which to base a group discussion.
- Write down points that you're unclear about as you read and bring them to the next group meeting for discussion.
- Draw up a plan to make sure that members of the group stay on topic. A different person could be responsible for the plan each week.
- Compare coursework and feedback to get as much information as possible about what the tutor is looking for.

Remember, if you don't feel that the group is working, you can always leave or meet less frequently. However, if everyone agrees on the aims early on and sticks to them, the group is much more likely to succeed.

Contribute to an online forum

An online forum is another way in which you can get support from others but without the commitment that a study group involves. However, this doesn't mean that there is no commitment at all. To get the most out of a forum you must make regular contributions, respond to messages and keep in touch with the other members. You could use the search words 'student online forum' to find a forum that suits you. One advantage of this style of communication is that you don't have to respond to someone 'on the spot' as in a study group. You can think carefully about your response before submitting it and in this way you might come up with more useful contributions. Don't be too trusting of answers in forums though as not all of them are reliable. Forums should not replace revision materials. Use them as a place to discuss topics and practise arguments but not as your main source of information or ideas.

Memory techniques (mnemonics)

Some people find memory techniques very useful, especially for exams in which formulae, dates and key words need to be memorised. Look at the examples below to see ways in which students use memory techniques and use them to come up with your own mnemonic.

Mnemonic for the symptoms of mania

Take the first letter of each of the symptoms and remember the 'word' that this creates. In the exam, recall the 'word' or 'words' and then this will remind you of the symptoms.

DIG FAST

D = Distractibility and easy frustration

I = Irresponsibility and erratic, uninhibited behaviour

G = Grandiosity

F = Flight of ideas

A = Activity increased with weight loss and increased libido

S = Sleep is decreased

T = Talkativeness

Mnemonic for the reactivity of metals

Form a sentence using the first letter from the different elements you need to remember:

Peaceful **s**ouls **c**an **m**ake **a** **z**ombie **i**n **t**he **l**onely **h**ot **c**ountry **m**ore **s**ympathetic.

P = potassium

S = sodium

C = calcium

M = magnesium

A = aluminium

Z = zinc

I = iron

T = tin

L = lead

H = hydrogen

C = copper

M = mercury

S = silver

Tips for top scores

- If you've been too nervous to ask questions in class, being a member of a study group provides a forum to find answers to those questions. Make good use of the opportunity to air any queries you may have.

- Leave margins around your notes so that you can add details from other sources that you read.

- Make up your own mnemonics. You'll remember them more easily if they use your own ideas.

✓ Dos	✗ Don'ts
✓ Become a proactive member of your study group. Participating will help you more than just sitting and listening.	✗ Continue to be part of a revision group if it isn't working for you.
✓ Make sure you're an active note-maker and use your own words.	✗ Get a false sense of security by writing copious notes without any clear focus.
✓ Write down questions to bring up at your revision group while you're revising on your own.	✗ Just memorise – you need to understand.
✓ Experiment when making notes to find out which style suits you best.	✗ Stick to one revision technique – variety will keep you motivated.

5 Looking after yourself

When it comes to revising for exams, it's important to remember to put yourself first. Think about strategies to boost your brain power and concentration when studying, while making sure you don't cut yourself off entirely from your normal routine and your friends and family. This means you'll have to spend some time thinking about how to get the balance right so that you can stay focussed but avoid letting your exams and revision take over your life.

Managing revision stress

It's a rare person who doesn't feel a certain level of stress before important exams. It has even been suggested that those who don't feel anxious actually perform less well than those who do. So it's only when stress starts to prevent you from revising that you really have to worry. (See the last section in this chapter for advice on how to cope if that's the case.)

Techniques for de-stressing

Try some of the following to help you take your mind off revision and exams.

- A complete break from your studies can be a good starting point. Watch a film or play a computer game.
- You may well benefit from physical exercise. Go to a dance class or for a run to clear your head.

Breathing techniques

Stress can make you start breathing with quick, shallow breaths and make your heart beat faster than usual. If this happens, sit down and place one hand on your stomach to check how quickly you're breathing. If it's one breath every couple of seconds, take a deep breath and start counting steadily. Breathe out slowly and try to get the last of the breath out after about five seconds. Carry on doing this until you're doing it naturally.

Relaxation techniques

Try these relaxation techniques to help you clear your mind at the end of the day or to give yourself a break.

- Close your eyes and breathe slowly and deeply
- Locate areas of tension and try to relax those muscles; imagine the tension disappearing
- Relax each part of your body, from your feet to the top of your head
- As you focus on each part of your body, think of warmth, heaviness and relaxation. Try and visualise a situation that helps you to feel calm, such as lying on a beach or chatting in a favourite place with friends.
- After 20 minutes, take some deep breaths and stretch.

Looking after your health

Taking care of yourself and making sure you keep healthy should be one of your top priorities while you're studying. Eat healthy food, drink plenty of fluids and have a good night's sleep every night. However, that's not always easy to do when your mind is on revision and exams. Read on to find out how to ensure you stay healthy while you're studying.

A well-balanced diet

To keep your brain in top condition you need a well-balanced diet made up of regular meals.

QUICK TIP

You might have read about so-called 'super foods'. Many of these foods have not had comprehensive clinical trials so it's more important to eat a well-balanced diet than rushing out to buy the food of the moment in the hope that it will help you achieve top grades.

On the Food Standards Agency website (www.food.gov.uk) you can find information about eating healthily while you're revising, as well as some quick nutritious recipes. One useful recommendation is to eat starchy foods while you're revising, such as:

- bread
- cereals
- rice
- pasta.

These foods should make up about one third of each meal and you'll benefit even more if you eat wholegrain varieties as they release energy more slowly to keep you going longer.

It's also important to eat iron-rich foods as these help to carry oxygen around the body and aid concentration. Eat red meat, green leafy vegetables and dried fruit to ensure that you get enough iron. If you usually snack on unhealthy foods, change to fruit while you're revising with only the occasional less healthy treat.

Follow these five top pieces of advice to help keep you healthy.

1. Eat a hearty, healthy breakfast – this will set you up for a day's revising.

2. Don't skip meals – your brain needs regular nourishment so you can concentrate fully on your revision.

3. Avoid junk food – it gives you an instant boost but then leaves you feeling lethargic and lacking energy.

4. Drink lots of water – dehydration makes you feel sleepy.

5. Cut down on caffeine – too much can make you feel anxious and keep you awake when you really do need to sleep.

Sleep

From the beginning of your revision period, establish a sleep routine and avoid staying up late revising night after night. A good night's sleep means at least six hours and many experts suggest that seven or eight hours is even better. Sleeping well benefits your brain and your concentration.

Study environment

Wherever you're studying, whether at home or university, you need to make sure you create a stress-free environment so that you can focus 100% on your revision.

If you have a choice of where to study (for example you have a revision week that gives you time to go home) think carefully about where you will study most effectively. Think about the resources available to you at home and at university and use the advantages and disadvantages in the chart below to help you to decide. Add or delete points to suit your own needs.

At home	At university
■ Don't have to worry about cooking meals.	■ University library close at hand.
■ Not enough privacy.	■ You can form study groups and get support from others on the same course.
■ Friends you've not seen for a long time might want to meet up.	■ You can arrange to see your tutor for extra advice.
■ Parents might put pressure on you to study more and this causes extra pressure or they may interrupt you and break your concentration.	■ Doing your own cooking gives you a chance to leave your desk for a while and helps you relax.
■ It's easier to relax when feeling tense in the familiar surroundings of your home.	■ You have a choice of where to study – the library or your room.
■ You can switch off by chatting with family members.	■ You're surrounded by other people who are revising.

If you find that the place that you've chosen for your revision really isn't working, then try somewhere else. There are fewer distractions in the library but you might feel more relaxed in your room so experiment with both. However, remember that it's not just the place that's important. Your revision strategies are the main key to success.

Wherever you are, there are some simple steps you can take to make your study environment conducive to your goal of achieving a top grade. Aim to feel comfortable but not too relaxed and try to have as many of the following as possible set up in your revision area:

- good lighting
- an ideal temperature (get a fan if you're too hot and wrap up if you feel cold)
- a comfortable desk and chair
- your revision materials close at hand
- as few distractions as possible
- a clock in the room – don't depend on your computer or phone to check the time as they might lead to distractions.

QUICK TIP

Remember: only you can decide the place that is best for you but remember that in your room your bed is always temptingly close at hand and once you decide to lie down and read on your bed, you'll need enormous willpower to stay awake. Some experts suggest having a study space that is separate from the place where you feel most relaxed is best.

Keeping yourself motivated

It can happen that you get to a point in your revision where you feel that you can't go on or that all the time you're spending on revision won't actually lead to the grades you're aiming for. Many people feel like this during revision and if you do reach a low point, you should have some strategies in place to pull you through.

To keep yourself on target, it helps to think about why you're in this situation – even though you're revising, stressed out and in a panic, you're doing it for a good reason. Ask yourself the following.

" *Why am I at university?* **"**

Think about why you came to university in the first place. You might have a love of your chosen subject or a dream of a future job that depends on a good degree. Either way, exams are a necessary part of the progress towards your future. When the exams are over and you've achieved good grades, you'll feel a real sense of achievement.

❝ *How will I reward myself when the exams are over?* **❞**

You can increase your motivation by planning something really special when the exams are finally over, for example, a holiday with friends, a party or meeting people you've hardly seen while you've been revising. Be realistic but at the same time make sure that your reward will do the trick.

Distractions

Even if you start off sticking to your revision timetable, you might find you're more easily distracted as the weeks pass, switching from revision to breaks more regularly or endlessly checking your phone and your emails to see what you might be missing.

If you find yourself in this situation, think of some encouraging words that will help to keep you going. Repeat these words every time you feel discouraged and give yourself a boost. Here are some examples:

- *'relax, concentrate, everything's going to be fine.'*
- *'exams don't last for ever – I'll be able to relax soon.'*
- *'there's light at the end of the tunnel.'*
- *'exams are never as bad as I think they are.'*

Tips to avoid distractions

- Switch off your phone – this may be difficult to do but it will vastly improve your concentration. Set a time for a break when you can switch it back on again and see who has been trying to contact you!
- Switch off your wireless connection – another difficult one but there will be no temptation to check the football scores, go onto a social networking site or download music.
- Shut your door – that way you won't be distracted by friends passing or your family going about their business.

You might think that by having even less contact with the outside world you'll become even less motivated. However, looking forward to going out with your friends once your exams are over is a reward that will help to keep you going in the long run. There are very few things in your social life that can't wait a few hours or days.

Signs that stress is getting the better of you

What are the signs that stress is becoming a problem? The list below indicates some of the features of stress and what you can do to relieve them.

- Are headaches a problem? Try going out to get some fresh air at regular intervals.
- Do you have problems going to sleep? Stop revising an hour before you go to bed and give your body a chance to change from study mode to sleep mode. Once in bed, relax your muscles from your head to your toes. Finally, visualise a situation where you feel really relaxed and listen to some quiet relaxing music.

- Have you lost your appetite? Wait until you're really hungry and go and buy something you really like.
- Are you always in a bad mood? Re-think your revision timetable. Maybe you need to have more frequent breaks.
- Do you feel tired all the time? Make sure you're having regular meals and that you stop revising while you're eating.
- Is lack of organisation getting you down? Get together with a friend and support each other.

Talking to people

If you experience some of the symptoms of severe stress you need to find ways to reduce your stress levels. There is a range of different people both on and off your university campus who can help you.

If you're at home and have a good relationship with one or both of your parents, tell them how you're feeling. They'll probably have noticed some changes in your behaviour and be glad that you've confided in them.

If you're studying away from home, you'll almost certainly have a student counselling service where you can see someone who has experience of helping students who are finding it difficult to cope with exams and revision.

Another person who can help you is your GP. If they think you need more support, they'll be able to suggest where to go and perhaps arrange an appointment for you.

Talking through your feelings will help to put problems into perspective and come up with solutions.

Tips for top scores

■ Treat your revision like a job. You don't take time off whenever you feel like it while you're at work. You stick to the breaks that are part of your daily routine. Do the same when you're revising.

■ Don't panic because your friends seem to be doing more revision than you. They might be trying to boost their confidence by appearing to be studying for 12 hours at a stretch but the reality might be quite different. If your revision plan is working, stick to it and ignore what other people are saying.

■ When you're relaxing, don't spend too much time with friends who you know are not focussing on their exams. You might find yourself becoming less focussed too.

✓ Dos	✗ Don'ts
✓ Establish healthy eating patterns to get you through the strains of the revision period.	✗ Leave it too late to find help if you feel really stressed: talk to people to help get some perspective on your concerns.
✓ Allow yourself treats from time to time.	✗ Depend on caffeine-laden drinks to keep you awake.
✓ Find a comfortable place to study where you can avoid distractions.	✗ Leave it too late to try a different location if you find your study environment isn't working for you.
✓ Learn to relax so that you can avoid becoming overly stressed.	

6 The day before the exam

When the day before the exam arrives, you'll start to wonder if you've revised the right topics and if you'll cope with the pressure on the day. Almost everyone feels like this and it's perfectly normal in the build-up to an important exam.

Now that you've completed your revision there are some final organisational steps to take to ensure success in your exam. You need to know that there's nothing you've forgotten to do and nothing you've forgotten to get ready. This means you have to stop revising and start preparing.

Checking the exam regulations

You'll be able to find the exam regulations for your university or college on their website. Read these carefully so that you know exactly what is expected of you in the exams.

The exam regulations outline what equipment you will be allowed in the exam room, and will delineate any other issues concerning behaviour or dress.

Here are some of the most common exam regulations you should be aware of.

- Normally you can't have a pencil case in the exam so you should put everything into a transparent plastic bag.
- Check your pockets before you sit down. You risk getting zero in the exam not only if your phone goes off but also if it's found on your person.

■ Many examination regulations won't allow you to wear any outer clothes, even a jacket. At a few universities there is a strict dress code for exams based on the traditions of the university so make sure you check to see if this could affect you.

You will **not** be able to have the following in the exam hall:

■ your mobile phone
■ your mp3 player
■ any pieces of paper or notes.

QUICK TIP
Don't take anything valuable with you that you'll have to leave in your bag outside, so you won't worry about it being stolen.

Equipment

The most common items of equipment you'll be able to take into the exam hall are:

■ pens and pencils – always take two of each in case they run out or break
■ pencil sharpener
■ rubber
■ ruler
■ highlighter pen(s)
■ calculator and other equipment specifically for mathematics and science exams
■ dictionary for foreign language exams
■ tissues
■ bottle of water
■ a watch – consider taking a watch even if you don't normally wear one. Many people check the time on their phone but you cannot take your phone into the exam. Even if there is a clock in the room, you might not be able to see it clearly from where you're sitting. You need to be able to keep an eye on the time.

Most important of all

YOUR STUDENT ID.

This will often need to be placed on the desk in front of you.

Get these items together the night before the exam so you don't have to worry about them on the actual day.

To cram or not to cram?

Last minute cramming is something that most people have done. It seems to make sense at the time, when you're looking for any way possible to perform better in the exam that is just around the corner. But does it really work?

If you study a large amount of material in a short time, research has shown that it's only kept in your short-term memory. This might work in some types of exam, for example a multiple-choice exam, but in most cases it won't be nearly as successful as starting to study earlier and storing the information in your long-term memory. Then you'll be able to make critical connections between different points and use these effectively in your exam answers.

Remember: examiners are looking for critical thinking in your exam answers, not memorised chunks from books. It's very difficult to have a full understanding of the material you're studying if you cram. Instead of cramming, review your summaries of your notes and any stickies you've made.

> **QUICK TIP**
> High grades come from understanding, not from memorising!

Getting enough sleep the night before

Almost everybody will advise you to get a good night's sleep – a minimum of six hours – the night before the exam. While no one can force you to get a good night's sleep, your brain, and therefore your concentration, will be affected if you try to manage on just a few hours. This will be even more detrimental if you have more than one exam in a week and you stay up half the night for the next one too! If you're not ready for the exam at this late stage, staying up all night or managing on only a few hours' sleep to do last minute revision is not really going to help.

QUICK TIP

Don't be tempted to stay up all night if you can't get to sleep. You'll get some rest just by being in bed. Remember not to drink too many caffeine-laden drinks during the day, try having a warm bath before going to bed and play some soft, relaxing music as you try to drop off.

Getting to the exam on time

It's surprising how many students don't arrive in time for the start of an exam. There are a number of reasons why they're late and it's important to avoid all of them. These include:

- sleeping in
- getting the time wrong
- delays on public transport
- not being able to find the exam hall.

THESE ARE PREVENTABLE!

Make sure you wake up in time

One of the last things you need to do to prepare for a morning exam is to ensure you have a system in place to prevent you sleeping in. All that revision will be wasted if you're more than a few minutes late as you'll be in a state of panic, have a reduced amount of time to do the exam and suffer from a lack of concentration because of the rush to get there.

You **MUST** have a foolproof way to wake up, especially if you didn't fall asleep until late because of worry. You're then even more likely to sleep in!

- Don't depend on your usual alarm – if you usually use your phone, use an alarm clock as well and if you usually use an alarm clock, think about having two!
- Don't use the snooze button – it's much too easy to go straight back to sleep again.
- Don't try staying up all night to avoid the risk of sleeping in.
- Ask someone really reliable to bang on your bedroom door or call you until you answer.

Check the time of the exam

- Go to the exams office and pick up an exam timetable or check online.
- Carefully transfer the information that applies to you into your diary or onto 'stickies' that you can see easily and use as reminders.
- Before going to bed, have a final check of the time and location.

Leave home in plenty of time

On a good day, you know how long it's going to take to get to where you're going. But what happens on a bad day?

Traffic jams, signal problems on trains, broken down buses and other unpredictable events can make you late for an exam. Don't let this happen to you. Get up early, eat a good breakfast (or lunch if it's an afternoon exam) and arrive in time to gather your thoughts and relax. After all those weeks revising, you owe it to yourself to be prepared on the day.

If you find that you're running late, it's important to keep calm. Most universities and colleges will allow students to enter an exam if they are up to an hour late. Rushing around in a panic won't help, so relax by taking deep breaths and work out your best course of action, even if this means taking a taxi.

Know where the exam will be

Sometimes exam halls are on a part of the university campus that you're not familiar with, or they could be in a public hall that is not on the campus itself. You must make absolutely sure you know where your exams will take place and if you haven't been to the building before, go there before the exam in case it proves difficult to find. You'll then know where the building is and how long it takes to get there.

> **QUICK TIP**
>
> Don't choose the day of an exam to try and impress your friends with what you're wearing. Wear clothes that you feel comfortable in and wear layers so that you can adjust to the temperature in the exam hall. You probably won't be able to keep your coat on and it's very difficult to concentrate if you're too cold – or too hot!

Last minute panic

It goes without saying that the best way to avoid a last-minute panic is to start your revision early, stick to your revision timetable and come to the exam feeling slightly nervous but not in a panic. However, even with the best intentions, you can get to the end of your revision and still feel that you're not really ready for the exam. So what can you do to overcome these last minute nerves?

- Think back to your relaxation techniques (see page 50) and put them into practice now.
- Don't think about past failures – now is the time to think you're going to do well.
- You don't have to be perfect – you can only do your best and if you're well-prepared you're in a good position to do this.
- As you stand waiting to go into the exam, ignore other people who are checking what they have revised with each other. If you join in this type of conversation, you might end up feeling confused or start to question your own preparation.
- Think about the reward that you're going to give yourself when the exam is over. It's only a few hours away!
- Eat a banana while you're waiting – it will boost your energy levels and release the energy slowly.

Tips for top scores

■ Get off your bus or train one stop earlier than usual. A walk will benefit you more than being jolted around by strangers and your brain will function better, but make sure you can still reach the exam in plenty of time.

■ Establish a sleep routine at the start of your revision period. It will be much easier to sleep well on the night before the exam if you do this.

■ If you don't want to feel isolated waiting to go into the exam, arrange to meet a friend who you can trust and who won't increase any sense of panic near the exam hall.

■ Plan to arrive about 30 minutes before the exam starts. Too early, and the nerves will start to build up. Cut it fine by not leaving enough time, and you'll start to panic because you might be late.

✓ Dos	✗ Don'ts
✓ Get enough sleep the night before the exam.	✗ Forget to take a watch to your exam.
✓ Double-check the time and place of your exam.	✗ Pay too much attention to what other people are saying outside the exam hall.
✓ Have a reliable alarm clock or friend to wake you up on the morning of the exam.	✗ Forget your student ID.
✓ Leave home in plenty of time.	✗ Put your pens and pencils in a pencil case – use a plastic bag.
✓ Use relaxation techniques if you start to panic.	✗ Sit your exam on an empty stomach.

PART 3

During and after the exam

Now you're ready for the final hurdle – the exams themselves! All that time spent on effective revision will make the exam hall less daunting than it would otherwise have been. But there are still important decisions to be made and techniques to think about, not only on the exam day but after the exam too. The final chapters will ease the stress of exam nerves and ensure that, from the moment you sit down at your desk in the exam hall to the results and beyond, you stay in control and achieve the results you deserve.

7 Exam technique

After all the weeks you've spent revising, it's now time for the exam itself. As you enter the exam hall and look for your desk, it could take a few minutes to adjust to your surroundings. If these are your first university exams, you might be in a hall you've never seen before and be surrounded by a sea of faces that you don't recognise. Sometimes more than one exam takes place in the same hall. This can be unsettling but your preparations for the exam will help you to settle quickly.

Exam hall procedures

When you enter the exam hall you must follow the instructions that are laid out in the exam regulations for your university or college. These are available on the university or college website and you should have read them beforehand so that you know:

- what you can or cannot bring into the exam hall
- the latest possible time you'll be allowed to enter the exam hall if you're late
- when you can leave the exam hall – even though it might be tempting to leave the exam early, it's better to go through your answers carefully in the extra time that you have remaining
- what to do if you need to go to the toilet in the middle of the exam.

Other things to remember.

- If you have special needs, it's most important that arrangements are made to allow extra time well before the exam. You should contact the Learning Support Unit of your university at the beginning of your first year for assessment. They will then make special arrangements for the exam period.
- Always stop writing immediately after you're told to put your pen down. You can be penalised for continuing to write after you've been told to stop.
- Avoid interacting with your friends by looking at them or trying to catch their attention. This could be seen as a form of cheating. Focus on yourself and try to forget about everyone around you.

QUICK TIP

Remember to leave your bag and coat where you've been told to leave them and remain silent as soon as you go into the hall. Don't turn over the paper until you're told to. Don't take the question paper out of the hall with you unless you've been told that you can.

Common exam errors

As soon as you sit down in your chair in the exam hall, especially if you feel nervous, make sure that you don't make any type of mistake that can lose you marks and ruin your chance of a good grade.

First, check you're in the right section of the exam hall and that you have the right exam paper. You may feel that this is somebody else's responsibility but just in case that person got it wrong, make it your responsibility as well.

Next, make sure that you write your exam number on the paper. In order to get a grade at all you'll need to be identified! It's unusual to write your name on the paper as the person marking the paper should not know whose paper it is. So the next point to remember is NOT to write your name on the paper when you're asked for your number! Some universities require students to seal down the flap on the answer book at the end of the exam so check if you need to do this.

Here are a few other points you should try to remember.

- Read the instructions and the questions carefully so that you know what you're being asked to do. Careless reading of the instructions and the questions can easily lead to a low grade.
- Don't leave out part of the question or only address it when you're writing the conclusion.
- If you make rough answers and then transfer them to the answer paper, don't leave this until the last minute or you could make mistakes copying them up or run out of time.
- When answering multiple-choice questions, don't make any extra marks on the paper as the machine marking it might mistake them for your answer.
- Never leave an answer blank, unless by choosing the wrong answer you'll lose points (as sometimes happens in a multiple-choice test).
- Stay on topic – drifting away from the focus of your answer may make you feel confident that you've written enough but it won't gain you extra marks, in fact it might cause you to lose marks.
- If you find yourself completely stuck, move on to another question but remember to return to that tricky question later.

Dealing with panic during an exam

If you start to feel a sense of panic when you're in the middle of an exam, you'll cope better if you've prepared yourself for the likelihood of this happening. You might start to panic because you have a memory block or you may feel that you just can't go on because your hand is so tired that you cannot keep writing.

If you have a memory block, close your eyes and take some deep breaths. You can sometimes forget even the most basic spellings or facts that you were completely clear about the night before the exam.

- Try and visualise your notes. This will often be enough to jog your memory.
- Try and remember other facts that are related to the one you've forgotten.
- Leave any words that you're having difficulty spelling and come back to them later. Make a note of the parts of your answer that you'll return to later. You don't want to waste time looking through your answer from start to finish. The same advice applies to an important fact that you can't remember. Leave it and come back to it later.

A panic attack

A real panic attack can have physical signs that you can recognise from the list below. If you feel like this, you can ask an invigilator to accompany you out of the room for a few minutes. A short break away from the exam room can help you to feel calm again.

Symptoms of a panic attack are similar to the physical signs of panic in other stressful situations.

- You might feel physically sick.
- Your hands could start to shake and become sweaty.
- Your breathing could be affected and you might feel faint.
- You might have uncomfortable stomach cramps.

What can you do if you get some of these signs of panic during an exam? First try some breathing techniques and remember that taking a few minutes to calm yourself down is not a waste of time. You'll make better progress in the remaining time if you're in control of the situation.

- First, take a long deep breath in with your eyes closed.
- Next, breathe out again slowly releasing the tension in your shoulders and hands.
- Continue breathing in this way until you start to feel calmer.
- Sit with your eyes closed for two or three more minutes before starting to write again.

> If you feel so ill that you cannot continue, tell one of the invigilators. Your university or college will have procedures that they follow in this situation.

Writer's cramp

Writer's cramp is common, especially as most coursework these days is word-processed rather than handwritten. Students today, therefore, easily get out of practice and find it difficult to write for two or three hours without a break. Before the exams, when you were using past papers as part of your revision, you practised timed answers and this will have built up the strength in your hands and wrists. In the exam itself, by putting your pen down for a few minutes, shaking your wrists and reminding yourself that this aching will disappear as soon as the exam is over, you'll be able to keep writing. Use the time when you're resting your hand to read through your answer or to plan the next answer

Cheating in exams

It goes without saying that anyone found cheating in an exam will face serious consequences. Nevertheless, there are always students who are willing to take the risk in order to get a higher grade. You can even find websites that tell you how to cheat and try to convince you that you won't get caught. Don't forget that invigilators can access these websites too and keep up-to-date with the latest methods of cheating. Look at the list below showing some of the consequences of cheating and convince yourself that cheating is never worth it.

- A mark of zero is awarded for the exam.
- You can fail the module that the exam is a part of.
- You can be expelled from the university.

So don't at any point think that this is a risk worth taking.

Tips for top scores

- Remember to number your answers clearly, especially if you don't follow the order on the exam paper.

- Never let your use of past papers lull you into a false sense of security about the exam. Read all the instructions carefully just in case anything has changed.

- Take as little as possible with you to the exam hall so that you can take off your coat, put down your bag and go to your table with the minimum amount of trouble. You'll then feel more relaxed.

- Often exams are in the hayfever season. If you suffer from hayfever make sure you have non-drowsy medication to take on the day and plenty of tissues.

✓ Dos	✗ Don'ts
✓ Check the exam regulations carefully before the exam.	✗ Forget to go to the toilet before going into the exam hall.
✓ Check your pockets before entering the exam hall in case you take in something prohibited by mistake.	✗ Leave anything in your bag that you might need for the exam.
✓ Practise breathing techniques before the exam so that you know what works for you.	✗ Think that by cheating you have a chance of improving your grade.
✓ Write practice answers to build up strength in your wrists.	✗ Turn over the paper before the examiner tells you that you can.
	✗ Leave the exam early – use this time to check your answers.

8 The exam paper

Seeing the exam paper on your desk, you'll be wondering what lies in store. Your preparation for the exam will mean that you've already looked at past papers and will be familiar with the format of the exam you're about to take. This will save you time and lessen your anxiety levels. However, you'll probably feel a certain amount of trepidation, especially if this is your first exam. As you turn over the paper, stay focussed and stick to the plans you established while you were revising.

Reading the instructions

Most people feel quite nervous when they turn over the question paper to see the questions, with the inevitable thoughts going through their head:

- *'Have I revised the right topics?'*
- *'Can I understand what I'm meant to do?'*
- *'What if I can't answer any of the questions?'*

So what should you do first? Don't even think about starting to write on the piece of paper in front of you before you're completely clear about what you have to do. There's one exception to this rule and that's writing down some key facts/points/formulae that you've memorised if you're worried you might forget them. This is fine as long as you then put them to one side and think about the instructions in more detail.

Before you begin writing you should do the following.

- Read the question paper in full – make sure you turn it over to check you haven't missed anything. This may seem obvious but you'd be surprised how many students fail exams because they didn't read part of the question paper.
- Look at the start and finish time and decide how many minutes you're going to allocate to each question. Remember to give yourself time to read through your answers at the end. Jot down your timing plan somewhere so that you can easily see it as you're writing.
- Check how many questions you have to answer.
- Note whether the questions are all worth the same number of points, especially if your exam consists of questions broken into several parts.
- Read all the instructions very carefully. Do you have to answer questions from more than one section? If you answer the wrong questions, you're very likely to fail the exam. Many universities allow you to raise your hand to ask an invigilator for help if you don't understand what to do. Some will have a member of your department available for the first 10 minutes of the exam to answer routine questions but you won't be able to ask questions about the contents of your answer.

Analysing and choosing questions

Now that you've read and understood the instructions, you're ready to choose which questions to answer. You need to choose carefully in order to select the questions that are most likely to lead to good scores.

Work your way through these key stages.

1. **Read:** read **all** of the questions carefully before deciding which ones to answer.

2. **Highlight:** highlight the framing words before deciding which questions to answer.

3. **Think:** before making your final choices, think about how the questions fit in with your revision preparation.

4. **Select:** select the questions that you understand fully and that cover the topics that you've revised.

Many students rush to start writing the answer to their first question so you might feel rather anxious about your timing and be tempted to start writing too. However, it really is worth reading all the questions first. It can be tempting to skim the questions, find one that's on the topic that you've spent a lot of time revising and start writing straight away. This could prove to be a false economy. Questions need to be analysed to ensure that you understand them fully. It's therefore important to highlight or underline the topic words and equally important to do the same for the framing words.

Remember that essay answers don't require you to regurgitate the chapters of a book that you've memorised. You have to apply that knowledge to respond to the question. Even if you know a great deal about the topic, the question might not be a good choice because you don't fully understand what you have to do. If you can't understand the question properly, you won't be able to use your knowledge appropriately and this will almost certainly affect your grade.

As you read through the questions, you could use a coding system to help you to decide which questions to answer. This can be a simple system of letters or stars as in the examples below.

Good choice	G	***
Possible choice	P	**
Too difficult	D	

It's a good idea to eliminate the questions that you know you can't answer to get them out of the way first. With those that are left, divide them into two groups – the ones that you think you can answer and the ones you'll keep in reserve. Then think back over your revision and the framing words used before making your final choice.

So you've read the questions carefully and chosen which questions to answer. So what's next? It's time for some planning.

Planning your answers

By now you're probably beginning to wonder if you'll ever have time to write the answers to the questions but the steps you've just covered don't take as long as you might think – five or 10 minutes should be enough. The final step to take for each question is to make an outline plan.

The importance of planning

It's important to plan before you start writing to make sure that you stay on topic and that your answer is well-structured. Your examiner has to mark many essays and you want yours to be the one that stands out because it's concise and responds to the question. At this stage you'll be deciding what to include and, equally important, what to leave out. Your plan doesn't need to be lengthy – just enough to guide you through your answer so that you're not crossing things out and losing track of where you've got to. Your plan should save you time in the long run. An essay that includes waffle and padding will irritate the marker. More doesn't equal better! It could even happen that if you run out of time – which hopefully won't happen – the examiner will have a look at your plan and give you credit for the parts that you did not have time to include in your essay.

Example plan

Introduction
- background information
- thesis statement

Main point 1
- supporting evidence
- supporting evidence
- evaluation of evidence

Main point 2
- supporting evidence
- supporting evidence
- evaluation of evidence

Main point 3
- supporting evidence
- supporting evidence
- evaluation of evidence

Conclusion
- summary of main points
- overall response to question

Thesis statement

A thesis statement is usually the last sentence in the introduction to an essay answer. It's not a summary of the essay but shows the position you'll take in your response to the question. The paragraphs of your essay will provide evidence to support your thesis in the form of an academic argument. A well-constructed thesis statement will help you to stay on topic and guide the reader through your answer.

Order in which to answer questions

Another point to consider is the order in which you'll answer the questions. Should you tackle the hardest one first or the easiest? There are advantages and disadvantages of both strategies. Look at the suggestions below and think about which technique suits you best.

Writing the answer you think will be **easiest** first:

- you'll probably feel more confident and this might lead to a more positive feeling about the exam as a whole
- you might have so much to say that you forget to watch the time and you suddenly notice that you haven't left sufficient time to answer the other question/questions to the best of your ability.

Writing the answer you think will be **hardest** first:

- by getting this question out of the way, you'll have a sense of relief and be able to focus more easily on the questions that you think will bring you higher scores
- you might become so bogged down in trying to answer the question that you become worried about your ability to pass the exam and this could have a knock-on effect on your other answers.

The examiner is on your side

Remember that the examiner is not trying to lead you into a trap. You're being given the chance to show your response to the course and to demonstrate your strengths.

If you're writing essay style answers you should follow the same structure as an essay written as coursework. However, the examiner won't expect as much detail.

Look at the list below. These are some of the key points that examiners will be thinking about when they are marking exams.

- An answer that focuses on the question – your answer should not drift away from the specific response that the question suggests.
- An analysis of the most important issues – you won't have time to include everything you know in your answer so identify the key points that respond to the question most effectively, before starting to write.
- Evidence of having read and understood relevant literature – while it's not necessary to include direct quotations you should refer to the key texts related to the question.

- Use of examples that support your argument.
- Appropriate academic style – you should write in an impersonal, objective style, using language precisely and accurately. You should also avoid colloquial words and expressions.
- A consistent, coherent thesis which exhibits the ability to think critically and reason logically.

Timing your answers

While you're writing:

- don't forget to keep checking the time!
- don't forget to keep referring to your plan!

Those valuable minutes you spent at the beginning of the exam will have been wasted if you forget to do what you set out to do.

You've been given the amount of time that the examiner thinks that you need to write effective answers. If you finish the exam much too early, you have probably not included all the points that are necessary to achieve a good grade. As you finish each answer, leave a space before starting the answer to the next question so that you can add more later if you have time to spare. If you only have a short time left at the end of the exam, use this time to re-check your answers. Students who leave the exam room early are not usually super-efficient at answering questions; it's more likely they have not prepared properly.

QUICK TIP
Medical evidence suggests that your brain, and therefore your grade, will benefit if you have a drink of water from time to time. So pause, have a drink and collect your thoughts. Your arm will get a welcome break too!

Tips for top scores

- You have a much better chance of a top score if your answers to each essay style question are approximately the same length (if the questions are equally weighted). Bear this in mind when planning your answers.

- You should show evidence of extensive background reading in your answers and be able to understand the problems and limitations of the different arguments.

- In the thesis statement in your introduction, show the examiner that you fully understand the question by focussing on your response, don't merely repeat the title.

✓ Dos	✗ Don'ts
✓ Read the questions carefully.	✗ Panic when you first look at the questions.
✓ Answer the correct number of questions.	✗ Automatically think everyone else knows more than you just because they begin writing immediately.
✓ Make plans and stick to them.	✗ Be over-ambitious and run out of time.
✓ Write legibly.	✗ Tell the examiner everything you know, focus only on what has been asked for.
✓ Try and relax.	
✓ Keep an eye on the time.	

9 After the exam

Finishing an exam brings a sense of relief. Even if you're worried about your performance, you can learn from your mistakes and move on. When you've finished all of your exams, there is even more to celebrate and you deserve this celebration. However, as well as rewarding yourself for all your hard work, you also need to think about how well your revision strategies worked and what you'll do differently next time. You need to think about these things now – don't leave it until the next set of exams comes around!

Post-mortem after exams

When students leave an exam hall there is usually a babble of conversation as people meet up with friends and discuss how the exam went. This is a natural thing to do and it acts as a way of 'letting off steam' after all the stress of the exam process. However, it can also be discouraging as you listen to how other students answered the questions and you can easily feel a sense of despondency, thinking that you've missed some of the key points, misinterpreted a question, or just not performed as well as the others. On the other hand, you might be the one feeling that it went well while others are worried about their performance.

Either way, it's best to remember that you can't do anything about the exam that has just finished, but there is time to work on improving your performance in the next one. So whether you have more exams to come or you've finished your last exam, it's better to avoid post-mortems and move on. You won't find out how well you've done until the exam results are published and there is nothing you can do in the meantime. Only the examiner knows what is expected in the answers and discussing your answers with your friends won't reveal this.

Time to relax

Even though it's better not to discuss the exams that you've finished in too much detail with your friends, you'll almost certainly want to see friends and relax. Now is the time to catch up with people you haven't seen for a while, to take part in activities that you had less time for while revising, spend time with your

QUICK TIP

Only talk to people you really trust straight after an exam. When the adrenalin is still flowing, you shouldn't take what others are saying too literally.

family and give yourself the rewards that you decided to have on finishing the exam. In other words, relax and enjoy yourself before starting the cycle of revision all over again.

The amount of time you can afford to spend relaxing depends on your exam timetable. If you have another exam coming up soon, a revision-free afternoon will have to do and no more than a day if your next exam is further away.

Moving on to the next exam

You can think about each exam that you take as being part of a learning curve. To make the most of being in this situation, you must re-visit your revision period and think about which techniques helped you and which were less successful.

QUICK TIP

Although it might be tempting to destroy your notes after an exam it makes sense to keep them just in case you have a resit.

You'll have to think about each exam and if you think you did badly, or if your grades show that you did badly, sit down in front of your computer or with a piece of paper and a pen and make some notes.

Review your exam techniques

Look at the checklist below and make notes under the headings that you think apply to you. Possible responses have been included to give you some ideas but your own answers could be quite different. When you've finished making your notes and thought about each point carefully, you'll have identified your problem areas and you can then return to previous chapters of this book in order to improve your exam techniques. Even though you don't have the results yet, you'll benefit from going through these steps soon after the exam.

If you do get your results and find that you've achieved good grades, you should never become complacent and think that you've mastered the technique of sitting exams. There is always room for improvement and by analysing your revision and preparation methods, you can aim for even better grades in the next round of exams.

Were my revision techniques effective?

YES + evidence	NO + evidence
I had covered all the key areas in the exam questions.	I did not start my revision early enough.

Did I recall the key points that I revised?

YES + evidence	NO + evidence
Most of my memory techniques worked well and I could use my background reading effectively.	I spent too much time cramming just before the exam and could not recall this information in the exam itself.

Did I run out of time?

YES + evidence	NO + evidence
Because I spent too long on the first question.	No, because I planned the time I would spend on each question at the beginning of the exam.

Did I have time left after I finished writing all the answers?

YES + evidence	NO + evidence
I did not revise enough and ran out of things to say.	I timed my answers well and left enough time to read through my answers at the end.

Did I follow all the exam procedures and the instructions on the paper?

YES + evidence	NO + evidence
I took only things I was allowed to have with me into the exam hall.	I forgot to take a spare pen and my pen ran out.

Did I understand all of the questions?

YES + evidence	NO + evidence
I looked at past papers while I was revising.	I did not pay enough attention to 'framing' words while I was revising.

After each exam, go through these questions again and see if you learnt from the mistakes that you made previously.

Waiting for the results

It's never an easy time waiting for exam results but worrying at this stage is not going to help you to get a better grade. Now is the time to focus on yourself, to have fun and to relax. You certainly deserve a break from the stresses of the revision period and exams. Before leaving the exams behind though, you should find out when your results are due from your university or college. Ask in the department before leaving for home or check on their website.

You also need to know where you can access your results. Many universities and colleges have an online results system where all your results from the semesters and the exams will be made available to you. Others may post your results or send them to your personal email account. Find out what your university or college does so that when results' day arrives, you know exactly how you can access your grades.

What happens if you fail?

Even if you feel that you revised thoroughly for all your exams and that your exam techniques were carefully put into practice, there is still the possibility of failing an exam. Failing any sort of test or examination is always a disappointment and it's necessary to spend time thinking about the reasons. It could be something simple such as you were feeling ill on the day of the exam. In that case it will be easy to reassure yourself that the resit will go much better as long as you're well-prepared and in good health. However, there might be reasons that you're not clear about and you should try to find out what went wrong and why.

First think about your answers to the questions in the chart on pages 89–91 and then move on to the questions below.

❝ Did you do badly in most of your exams or just one of them? ❞

You'll need to analyse your exam and revision techniques thoroughly if you performed badly in all your exams. If you only failed one exam, you'll probably be able to work out more quickly what went wrong. For example, you may have missed one key topic when you were revising. Next time you need to ensure that your revision plan includes all the important topics.

❝ Are your grades for coursework also low or are they better than your exam grades? ❞

If your grades for coursework are good, then you can be reassured that you understand the key concepts but you're not able to use and apply this knowledge effectively in exam conditions. Using past exam papers might help you, especially if your tutor can check your practice answers. If your grades for coursework are also low, then you'll need to rethink your studying strategies. A good starting point would be the *Student Essentials: Study Skills* title in this series.

> ❝ *Did you use the same techniques that you used to use for school exams?* ❞

School exam answers are usually more descriptive than university exam answers. If you depend on the techniques you used at school, you'll often find that your answers did not include sufficient analysis.

Next, arrange an appointment with your tutor to discuss your exam (after checking that they have access to your paper, some don't). While you might not be able to see your actual exam paper, your tutor will probably be able to explain what went wrong. This advice is very important in order to avoid making the same mistakes again. Remember, tutors are often involved in other projects during the summer vacations, such as research or conferences abroad, so you'll have to find out when they are available.

Finally, be very honest with yourself. Did you really revise effectively when you were sitting at your desk during the revision period? It's easy to blame the exam or the marker for your grade but it's more likely that you slipped up somewhere during the revision period. Analyse where you went wrong so you can avoid making the same mistake in future.

QUICK TIP

Talking to a friend who achieved a good grade might also be helpful but the advice your tutor gives you will be more important.

Preparing for resits

If you fail an exam, most universities and colleges will allow you to resit it, usually towards the end of August. If you need to resit any of your exams, it's important to check the website of your university or college to find out the procedures for resits.

Each university has its own system but the following points will help you get an idea of what to expect.

- You'll probably have to pay a fee for each exam that you re-take.
- There is often a maximum grade that you can attain, for example 40% or 50% depending on the university.
- You're sometimes only able to resit one exam. If you've failed more than one exam, you might have to repeat the year.

You'll need to make a new revision timetable, learning from the mistakes that you made first time round. Resist the temptation to leave your preparation to last minute cramming because you've revised everything already. You might have to repeat the whole year if you fail again this time!

Don't forget to register for your resits. Contact the exam office as soon as you find out that you need to take an exam again. There will be paperwork to complete, an exam timetable to collect and perhaps revision classes to enrol for. Plan ahead and give yourself the best chance of succeeding second time around.

Motivating yourself to start revising all over again won't be easy, especially in the summer when all your friends are enjoying themselves and going on holiday. Just because you have resits looming, there is no reason for you not to have a holiday too. You need time to relax after the stresses of the university year and your exams, and in fact a holiday will enable you to return to your desk or the library feeling refreshed and ready to focus on your studies again.

Tips for top scores

- If worrying about your last exam is preventing you from focussing on the next one, find someone you trust to talk to or go to see a student counsellor.

- Take a note-book with you when you go to see your tutors about your results and take note of what they say. It's easy to forget important points later.

- If you're having trouble focussing on your resits, think about why you chose your subject and how your degree relates to your future plans.

✓ Dos	✗ Don'ts
✓ Take time to reflect on each exam when it's finished as preparation for the next exam.	✗ Believe everything other people say after an exam. You'll only know how well you've done when the results come out.
✓ Remember to give yourself a reward after each exam. It will motivate you to keep going.	✗ Let bad feelings about one exam affect your preparation for the next one.
✓ Contact your tutor if you need advice but remember that you might not get an appointment exactly when you want one. Try to be flexible.	✗ Spend the whole summer revising if you have resits. You need a rest just as much as everyone else.
✓ Register for any resits in plenty of time.	✗ Think that because you failed an exam first time round, you'll fail the resit too. Proactive preparation for the resit can make all the difference.

Revision and exam strategies Q&A

How can I resist the temptation to spend time with friends when I should be revising?

This can be very difficult but you should set yourself targets and see your friends as a reward for meeting your targets. Look at Chapter 1 for some ideas.

I don't think my revision techniques are really effective. Are there any other strategies I can use?

There are many different ways of revising from forming study groups to using an online forum. Find out what style suits you in Chapters 2 and 4.

How can I use past exam papers to help me revise?

Past exam papers can be used for more than just checking what came up last year. See Chapter 2 to find out more.

How can I work out what the examiner really wants me to do?

You won't know exactly what the examiner is looking for but you can look at marking criteria (look back at Chapter 2) and use your assignments to get a good idea.

My notes are always disorganised. How can I make clear notes?

There are many different styles of notes and in Chapter 4 you'll find one that suits you.

I feel so unhealthy when I'm revising. I don't want to waste time exercising and I seem to drink coffee all the time to stay awake. How can I stay healthy?

You're allowed to have breaks when you're revising and you can go jogging or to the gym. For hints and tips on how to stay healthy, see Chapter 5.

I hate the day of the exam itself and always seem to be disorganised. How can I avoid this?

Start your preparation in advance. You'll find more on this in Chapter 6.

I always seem to pick the wrong questions and this affects my grades. Is there something I can do to avoid this?

You can prepare in advance so that when you're in the exam with the paper in front of you, you'll have a system ready to help you choose the questions. See Chapter 7.

When I'm in the exam hall everyone seems to be writing much more than me. Is it important how much I write?

Your answer won't necessarily be better just because it's long. See Chapters 7 and 8 for advice on strategies when you're in the exam hall.

I never seem to learn from my past mistakes. What can I do to help prepare for my next exams?

In Chapter 9 you'll find strategies to help you go through what you found difficult and what you found less challenging so that you can work on improving your strategies for the next set of exams.

Glossary

Active revision
Active revision goes beyond reading books and making notes (see passive revision) and incorporates a variety of techniques to assist long-term memory.

Critical thinking
When you think critically, you need to identify and evaluate evidence to support an argument.

Exam regulations
Exam regulations are rules covering student conduct during exams.

'Framing' words
Framing words are used in exam questions to show you the direction your essay should take. Examples of framing words are 'evaluate', 'discuss' and 'analyse'.

Marking criteria
Marking criteria are bands showing what points are taken into consideration when grades are awarded.

Mnemonic
A mnemonic is a pattern of letters or association of ideas that help you remember something.

Mock exams
A mock exam is a practice exam that gives you a chance to write answers to questions that are similar to those that will be in the real exam.

Passive revision

Passive revision is associated with sitting at a desk, reading books and making some notes. This type of revision doesn't aid memory retention.

Past papers

A past paper is an exam paper from an exam that has already taken place. You can use past papers to help you prepare for exams.

Resit

A resit exam is taken if you failed the exam the first time. You're given a second chance and can take it again with new questions.

Synthesis

When you synthesise, you incorporate arguments from different sources written in your own words as the basis of a response to an exam question.

Thesis statement

A thesis statement is a sentence in an introduction, usually the last sentence, that presents your response to the exam question.

Virtual Learning Environments (VLEs)

Virtual Learning Environments give you access to learning and study materials online. Blackboard is a common VLE used by university tutors.

Viva

A viva, or *viva voce*, is an oral exam in which you discuss a piece of work with one or more examiners.

LEARN ALL THE ESSENTIALS

Including how to:

- ✓ Build arguments
- ✓ Use analytical techniques
- ✓ Create comprehensive arguments

STUDENT ESSENTIALS

Get to grips with core skills for critical thinking success

IN 1 HOUR

CRITICAL THINKING

Debra Hills